THE TOTALLY 100% UNO███ ██AL

ROBBIE WILLIAMS

• • • • • • • SPECIAL

£5.99

© 1999 Grandreams Limited

Written by Mick St Michael and Gaynor Betts
Designed by Jason Bazini

Published by
Grandreams Limited
435-437 Edgware Road
Little Venice
London W2 1TH

Printed in Belgium

CONTENTS

LET HIM ENTERTAIN YOU!

Robbie Williams is, contrary to early speculation, far and away the most successful of the five ex-members of Take That. Though initially Gary Barlow was expected to make the smoothest transition from teen idol to solo star and Mark Owen, the cute one, was the first to release an album, it was the joker in the pack who came up trumps. Robbie, the first to leave the band, released one of the most successful albums of 1997 in 'Life Thru A Lens', and at the end of 1998 saw the much-awaited follow-up, 'I've Been Expecting You', flying off the shelves.

Robbie has found his market – and it's a far wider fan base than just ex-Take That fans. More than that, his on and off relationship with Nicole Appleton has filled more gossip columns than you can shake a stick at. And, despite leading this busy but happy life, he still has time for his mother and in true 'Smashy and Nicey' style does a lot of work for charity.

This is Robbie's story – enjoy it!

DIARY OF A
SUPERSTAR

A history of Robbie Williams – from childhood to stardom and beyond

13 February 1974

Robert Peter Williams is born to mother Jan and father Pete Conway. In the same year, his comedian dad won the final of TV's *New Faces* talent contest. At the time, Robbie's parents ran a pub in Stoke-on-Trent, not far from the football ground.

1977

Having separated when Pete went off in search of fame, Rob's mum and dad divorce this year. His mum would ultimately give up the pub licence, but not before Rob had a chance to throw £2,000 out of the window! Jan, Rob and older sister Sally moved in with Robbie's nan – and, with three older females in the house, little wonder Rob is still in tune with his feminine, more sensitive side! His mother ran a successful ladies' fashion shop, an up-market cafe and then a florist. Today she is a drugs counsellor and still the most important person in Robbie's life.

1979

Rob starts his education at Mill Hill Primary School, Tunstall, Stoke-on-Trent.

1985

He attends St Margaret Ward High School, Tunstall. Always the joker, Robbie's school career wasn't an academic success. 'I wish I'd worked harder. Even though I hated the lessons, I loved school. I used to go for a laugh because I had such fun and I went to learn about life not to find out what *x* equals.' Conrad Bannon, the Headmaster of St Margaret

Ward, remembered his ex-pupil as 'bright, lively and the life and soul of his class. He wasn't shy, he was a real extrovert.' However, Robbie's memories of one of his teachers, hidden in poem form at the end of 'Life Thru A Lens', are somewhat less favourable!

1990

He works for a while as an assistant in his mum's florist shop and then as a bad double-glazing salesman, employed by his older sister's boyfriend. 'I just used to tell people they were over-priced and leave.' His mum then saw an ad in the *Sun* for a fifth member for a new boy band – then a relatively original idea – and encouraged Robert (as she always calls him) to apply. When the news came through that he was in, Rob screamed from his bedroom window that he was going to be famous. But things weren't that glamorous: the lads travelled around Britain in a beaten-up Escort, staying in seedy bed and breakfast establishments, and at times it looked as if they would never succeed.

1992

About a year and a half after Take That had been formed they play an under-18s club in Hull, and their market was identified – teenage girls began screaming in a frenzy. They were finally about to hit the big time, with a string of Number 1 hits to follow. Their phenomenal success is well documented, their faces blu-tacked to many a bedroom wall. ▶

DIARY OF A
SUPERSTAR

17 July 1995
Robbie and Take That part company. A press release announced, 'Robbie Williams is to leave chart-topping band Take That. He has left the group as he was no longer able to give Take That the long-term commitment they needed.' It happened just days before the Nobody Else '95 Tour, and Rob still claims that he was sacked. He had already told the lads at a band meeting the previous week that he was

album deal. In interviews he told how easy it was to write songs and how his debut album was going to blow everyone's socks off. Luckily it turned out to be true, but at the time Robbie hadn't created a single recordable track!

July 1996
Robbie appears at Capital Radio's Summer Music Jam, on London's Clapham Common, playing to a

handing in his six months' notice, intending to leave when his contract was up after their US tour. Litigation followed with both RCA (Take That's label) and Nigel Martin-Smith (their manager). Robbie had been a teenage millionaire, but would lose it all in court.

June 1996
Rob signs to Chrysalis Records for a £1 million, three-

50,000-strong crowd. He performs *Freedom*, released that month, his first live gig since leaving Take That. *Freedom* is released three weeks after Gary Barlow's debut solo single *Forever Love*. Barlow's track hits the top, while Robbie's effort peaked at Number 2, kept off the top by the Spices. The cover version of the George Michael track did not appear on his first album, it was simply a bid to remind people he was still on the scene – and no doubt to steal some of ▶

DIARY OF A SUPERSTAR

Barlow's thunder! The concert served to remind Rob what he did for a living and, with a little help from family, friends and a patient record company, he made moves to get his life and career back on track.

October 1996
Robbie spends the next few months climbing on and falling off the wagon as he seeks help from 'therapist to the stars' Beechy Colclough and checks into a rehab centre.

September 1997
'Life Thru A Lens' is released, the songs written by RW and Guy Chambers. Initial sales were disappointing at only 38,000 copies, but the release of the single *Angels* changed all that. Robbie emerged as a more rounded artist with a more adult sound, appealing to a more mature audience.

October 1997
Robbie launches his first solo 14-date nationwide tour and, against all odds, proves to be one of the best performers of his generation.

December 1997
Robbie and Gary make their peace in public at the Princess Diana Concert of Hope when both perform their solo tracks and join in the finale of *Let It Be*.

January 1998
He starts dating 'saintly' singer Nicole Appleton.

June 1998
Robbie plays the first pay-per-view concert from Sky TV, *Robbie Williams Live At The Forum*. It was introduced by showbiz pal Chris Evans. Robbie appeared in a number of ads trailing the event, whereby Robbie goes down a street door to door offering to sing. Unrecognised by the first few residents, he was finally invited in to perform in someone's front room. In the same month, he wins a Nordoff-Robbins award for Best Newcomer.

Autumn 1998
Robbie reaches number 85 in *Mojo* magazine's 'Top 100 Artists of All Time' poll. He was also number 100 in *Q*'s '100 Richest Stars In Rock 'n' Roll'; future polls are likely to see his rating rise.

October 1998
Robbie accepts *GQ*'s Solo Artist of The Year award, beating Gary Barlow and George Michael. He releases his new eagerly-awaited album 'I've Been Expecting You', which enters the UK chart in pole position.

November 1998
Robbie gets three nominations for 1998 MTV European Music Awards: Best Album, Best Male and Best Song. He wins Best Male. His acceptance speech is commendably concise: 'Damn right too!'

PERSONAL FILE

Robbie's intimate details under the spotlight

Name:	Robert Peter Williams
Birthdate:	13 February 1974
Birthplace:	Stoke-on-Trent, Staffordshire
Eye colour:	Green
Hair colour:	Brown
Starsign:	Aquarius
Distinguishing marks:	A tattoo of a Celtic cross on his right thigh
Earliest ambition:	'To be famous!'
Likes:	Being on stage 'and having all those girls screaming and shouting and throwing their knickers at me!'
Dislikes:	Violence. 'I'll do anything to protect my face.'
Perfect woman:	Nicole Appleton…'I love her to bits!'

Robbie the Actor

The young Robbie Williams had no ambition to be a pop star – he wanted to be an actor. A member of the local amateur dramatics club, he played the Artful Dodger in *Oliver*. He would still like to act and believes it can work with his music career, but for the moment music has to take precedence. There is a rumour that he was approached for the role of Renton in *Trainspotting*. He turned down a film with Harvey Keitel because he was busy recording the first album.

Robbie the Poet

Robbie's a bit of a poet and even planned on writing a book called 'Bob Through The Kitchen' – a title inspired by the fact that as a celebrity he always has to arrive the back way, through the kitchen. 'Poetry has got this bad reputation. It's a bit poncey and pretentious.' He introduced himself to Pulp at Glastonbury by reciting one of his poems.

Robbie the Animal Lover

Robbie loves his white Siamese cat. She was stolen when she was six months old but found on a stall in Notting Hill, up for sale for £10. Eventually man and kitty were reunited by the RSPCA .

Robbie the Weightwatcher

Robbie confesses to always having had a weight problem. He was first teased about his puppy fat when he was on the beach at the age of four and some lads were laughing at him. Rob claims this is his earliest memory (shame!). He realised early on as a schoolboy that he could placate bullies with humour and be popular with his school friends. 'I was this chubby boy who would pull faces and tell jokes and I got a big circle of friends.'

During his time with Take That the manager sent him letters; they apparently didn't speak to each other for the first two years, threatening to kick him out of the band if he didn't lose weight. He drank

because he was depressed about his weight and feeling isolated after the split from Take That. He also saw getting fat as rebelling against the harsh regime run by Martin-Smith. He was described by one music publication at the time as 'a drug-guzzling, champagne-dribbling, bloated tabloid buffoon, affectionately known as Blobby'. Ultimately he is happier and feels better without the booze and the added weight.

Robbie the Psychic

Robbie has a very psychic side and claims, 'Me mum's a white witch! She reads Tarot cards, she reads palms.' He says it is his psychic side that chose Guy Chambers from a list of people he could choose to collaborate with. 'I've been psychic all my life. It can be very scary as I pick up bad vibes.'

He also follows the art of Feng Shui, positions his furniture accordingly and always remembers to put the loo seat down – the theory being that otherwise your money is symbolically flushed away.

Robbie the Ghostbuster

In the past Robbie has moved house because of ghosts. He was living with his girlfriend at the time in Belsize Park, London, when he felt spirits move through him.

Apparently doors banged and tape decks were turning off and on, and Rob did a runner to the nearest hotel.

TOTALLY 100% **UNOFFICIAL**

THE TAKE

A mega-rich superstar at sweet sixteen...

Rob was picked for Take That on the same day he failed all his GCSEs, following a short but disastrous spell as a double-glazing salesman. He responded to an ad in the *Sun* to be the fifth member of a band created by manager Nigel Martin-Smith, along the lines of America's very successful New Kids On The Block. Rob, however, always considered himself an outsider in the band and maintains that Martin-Smith never liked him.

Jason Orange and Howard Donald were already working as break-dancing duo Streetbeat, while Mark Owen and Gary Barlow had worked together in the Cutest Rush, a group funded by money Barlow won from winning the BBC's *Song For Christmas* competition. Rob, their youngest member, was new to showbusiness and dance routines; he learned the ropes, but perhaps could have done with a little more understanding and patience.

TOTALLY 100% **UNOFFICIAL**

THAT YEARS

Memories of his spell with the top boy band in the land

Rob sang Jason Donovan's *Nothing Can Divide Us* at the audition. 'I remember the first time I ever met the lads at the Take That auditions. I came with my mum and I was saying through the corner of my mouth. "Right, Mum – go now." Marky was doing exactly the same thing at the other end of the street with his mum.' Having met the other lads, Rob recalls them as being weird and thinking, 'I wish I'd passed my exams!'

Rob now claims that Gary always amused him. 'Then Gary called me over and said, "Right, son – here's what you do." He called me "son"! He made me laugh from that moment on.' The band performed a showcase for the press at Hollywood's nightclub in Romford, then being presented as a leather-clad dance troupe. The focus, of course, would change as a teenage audience discovered them, and Gary Barlow's songwriting hit its stride. Gold records and mountains of acclaim followed – but what exactly was going on behind the scenes?

Certainly, Rob was clearly far from content.

Immediately after the split he launched a scathing attack on the band, particularly Gary. He claims to have spent six years trying to get Gary's approval before he finally gave up on Take That. Rob was also reported as having labelled his former partners as 'selfish, greedy, arrogant and thick'. He is quoted as saying, 'I never liked them. I definitely felt manipulated from the off. From day one I was being deliberately ostracised.'

Partly, no doubt, because he felt like an outsider, Rob always seemed to take a back seat in the band's business decisions. He played the joker as a defence mechanism and in the hope that it would make him liked.

Despite Gary's problems with Rob, explaining that no-one can get any sense out of Rob in the studio, he admitted that while the other band members practised their vocals, Rob would lounge on the sofa, then 'do his vocals perfectly straight away'. Rob himself admits that he never actively expressed a view on decisions made about the band. 'I wished I'd realised that I was in a better ▶

THE TAKE THAT YEARS

bargaining position… I wished I'd used that when I was in a group, that I'd spoken up more.'

At the height of the band's fame their record company was receiving 10,000 phone calls from fans every week. 'Life provided a lot of new things that were very dangerous and seductive. I was in a position to do almost anything I wanted, when I wanted,' recalls Rob. The downside included pressure on Rob's home life; his mum's florist shop closed because customers were put off by the fans hanging around. She also had a nightmare selling her home, with fans making appointments to view just to get a glimpse of Rob's bedroom. Gifts from her son of a better house and a BMW convertible no doubt eased the frustrations.

The pop star regime, which meant a can of regular (non-diet) cola was a treat, the constant sycophancy and bodyguard accompaniment, eventually wore Rob down. 'I would put a cigarette in my mouth, and seven people would try to light it for me. It began to get really tiresome.'

It was Robbie's jaunt to Glastonbury in 1995 which finally put an end to that lifestyle. Rob was advised that if he went he should take a security guard to prevent any unofficial photographs being taken. He had been similarly accompanied the previous year and, as a consequence, spent most of the festival hiding inside M-People's tour bus. This time he wanted to have fun and see Oasis, his favourite band.

He borrowed 16 bottles of champagne from a Nordoff-Robbins reception he was attending, loaded them into the boot of his Jag and drove to Glastonbury. By all accounts he had a fabulous time, doing every unofficial interview on offer and dancing with Oasis on stage. Rob himself can't actually remember much about it, but the repercussions are still crystal clear in his memory.

As far as the band was concerned it was the straw that broke the camel's back. Rob may have given six months' notice, but he left with immediate effect. He maintains that he was fired and still regrets that he didn't get to do one last tour and say goodbye to the fans.

Take That officially disbanded on 13 February 1996, Rob's birthday. Following one suicide in Germany, counselling phone lines were set up for fans across Europe. Everyone seemed to be getting support, except for one rather confused and increasingly bitter ex-group member. When asked to comment, he said, 'I did my grieving when I was kicked out. Frankly I'm more concerned with how Port Vale do in the Cup tonight. Anyway, it's my birthday and I'm off to celebrate.' Since leaving Take That Rob has said a lot about his former 'friends'. Many of these comments he now regrets, putting it down to bitterness during a year when he was rebelling from the strict regime of the band and ▶

THE TAKE THAT YEARS

almost went off the rails. He described Gary in one rather rude, four-letter word and compared his time with the band as a prison sentence. His opinion of his ex-manager doesn't appear to have changed much. On 'Life Thru A Lens's sleeve, he says, 'Nigel Martin-Smith, I think of you a lot and my past is something I find difficult to accept, especially the part with you in it…', but he has withdrawn many of his other anti-Take That comments. 'I had six brilliant years with Take That, but for the last year all I could remember was the nasty ending. But now the good times are coming back to me and, more than anything,

I'd love to have a good chat with Gary.'

Rob admits Gary came across as the bigger man post-Take That. He could have fought back at Rob's not-so-subtle attacks, but either remained silent or praised Rob as the best performer in the band. 'It was a very high compliment and I know that he meant it. While I've been spouting my mouth off, he's kept himself together, even though I've tried very hard to rattle his cage.'

It is Mark who Rob has always been closest to, calling him his confidant and buddy. 'I'd love him to ring me up and say, "Rob, you're right – that Nigel is a ****. Let's go out for a drink and slag him off." But I doubt he ever will. That's not Mark's style.' It was only Mark who spoke to Rob when the remaining members played at the BRIT Awards the February after Rob left. While the others turned away, Mark waved and called, 'Look after yourself'. Rob would like to patch things up with all the boys, explaining, 'I'm sick of fighting, I just want to see my mates again…'

On the whole era, he concluded, 'The Take That story will go down as a valid chapter of pop history. The band made some good throwaway pop, and I'm a great fan of pop. *Back For Good* is a brilliant song. There – that probably destroys the "Robbie hates Take That" myth!

'I'm going to be that successful again, only this time I'm going to be able to breathe and enjoy it.' This certainly appears to be the case, not only in Rob's own opinion but in the opinion of many others. Since the split, Madame Tussaud's have made a wax work of Gary Barlow, initially believing he would be the biggest solo artist to rise from the ashes of the group. However, a spokesperson said that they are currently considering making a Robbie model…

STARRING ROLE

Do you want the low-down on Robbie's starsign?

Our stargazer reveals all!

Robbie's Starsign: Aquarius (The Water Bearer)
21 January to 19 February
Ruling planet: Uranus
Birthstone/colour: Turquoise

Aquarians are often:
Friendly and humanitarian, honest and loyal, original and inventive, independent and intellectual

On the darker side, they can be:
Stubborn and contrary, perverse and unpredictable, unemotional and detached

Aquarians often like:
Fighting for causes
Dreaming and planning for the future
Thinking of the past
Good companions
Having fun

Aquarians often dislike:
Empty promises
Loneliness
The ordinary
Imitations
Idealism

Other Famous Aquarians:
Author Charles Dickens (7 February 1812)
TV comedian Benny Hill (21 January 1924)
Friends' Jennifer Aniston (11 February 1969)
'Baby' Emma Bunton (21 January 1976)
Aussie soap star Isla Fisher (3 February 1976)
US popster Nick Carter (28 January 1980)

Aquarians are strong and attractive personalities that divide into two types: one sensitive, gentle and patient; the other exuberant, lively and exhibitionist (guess which Robbie is!). Both are strong-willed and forceful and have strong convictions, though as they seek truth above all things, they are usually honest enough to change their opinions if evidence persuades them they have been mistaken.

They have a breadth of vision that can see both sides of an argument, making them tolerant of other points of view. They are nearly always intelligent, clear and logical. Many are imaginative and psychically intuitive.

Both types of Aquarian need to retire from the world at times, and appreciate opportunities for meditation. Even in company they are fiercely independent, refusing to follow the crowd. They dislike interference by others, however helpfully intended, and will accept it only on their own terms. They have good taste in drama, music and art, and are also gifted in the arts, especially drama.

Aquarians work best in group projects, provided they have a leading part in them. They have a feeling of unity with nature and a desire for knowledge and truth that makes many great scientists, especially astronomers and natural historians. On the arts and humanities side their progressive tendencies can be expressed in writing, especially poetry, and broadcasting, or as welfare workers and teachers. Some have gifts as entertainers and make good character actors (having an ability to mimic) and musicians. The more psychic among them possess healing gifts.

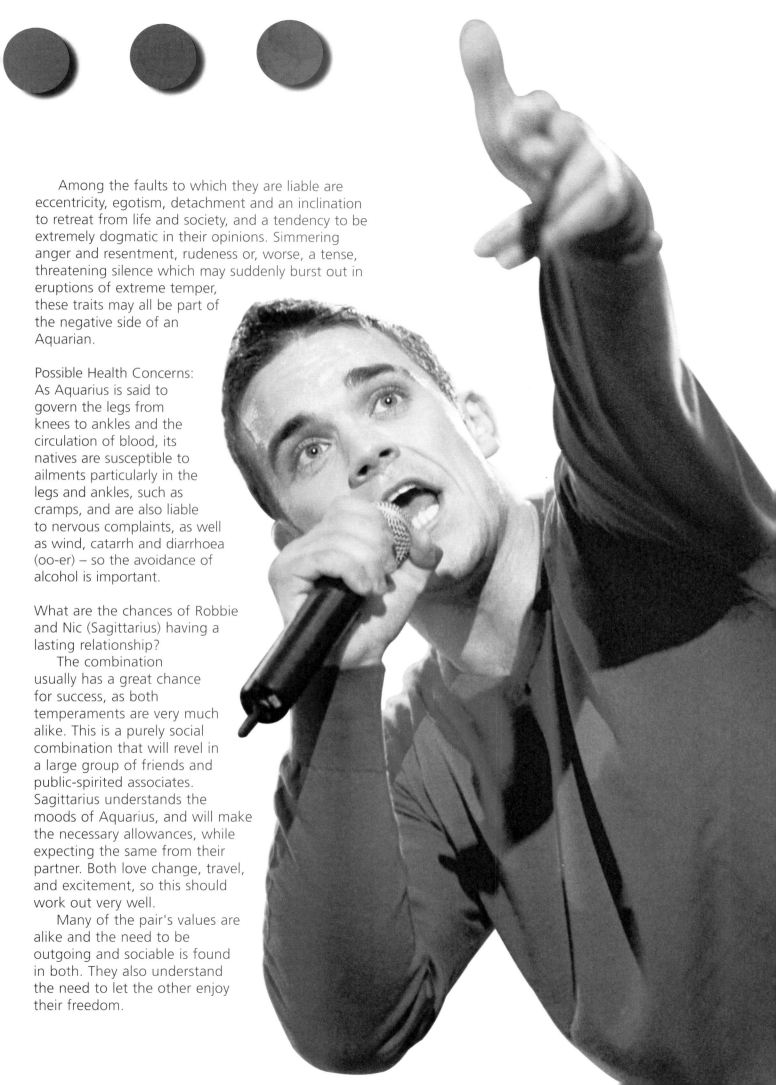

Among the faults to which they are liable are eccentricity, egotism, detachment and an inclination to retreat from life and society, and a tendency to be extremely dogmatic in their opinions. Simmering anger and resentment, rudeness or, worse, a tense, threatening silence which may suddenly burst out in eruptions of extreme temper, these traits may all be part of the negative side of an Aquarian.

Possible Health Concerns: As Aquarius is said to govern the legs from knees to ankles and the circulation of blood, its natives are susceptible to ailments particularly in the legs and ankles, such as cramps, and are also liable to nervous complaints, as well as wind, catarrh and diarrhoea (oo-er) – so the avoidance of alcohol is important.

What are the chances of Robbie and Nic (Sagittarius) having a lasting relationship?
The combination usually has a great chance for success, as both temperaments are very much alike. This is a purely social combination that will revel in a large group of friends and public-spirited associates. Sagittarius understands the moods of Aquarius, and will make the necessary allowances, while expecting the same from their partner. Both love change, travel, and excitement, so this should work out very well.
Many of the pair's values are alike and the need to be outgoing and sociable is found in both. They also understand the need to let the other enjoy their freedom.

Nobody can deny that Robbie Williams' love-life has been anything but entertaining. In the past few months it seems that Robbie and his latest romantic adventures have never been out of the media for long. And we all love to read the latest gossip. Admit it, who hasn't taken a second glance at the latest headline featuring our Rob? This is the story so far...

Mention the words 'Robbie Williams' and 'women' in the same sentence and the name 'Nicole Appleton' will not be far behind. Never has the phrase 'on and off relationship' been more applicable than to this pop pairing! Their relationship has been decidedly rocky...

Robbie and Nic began dating in January 1998, and six months later Rob asked her to marry him. The June proposal came as a surprise, as did the huge emerald engagement ring. But more was to come: she called off the engagement just seven weeks later in a phone call to Robbie when she was performing in Mexico, leaving Robbie devastated and in tears.

The plan had been to get married 'somewhere exotic' in 1999. 'The engagement is off,' Nicole explained to a friend. 'Robbie and I are no longer an item. Things just haven't worked out... I know we will always be close. But at the moment we just can't be together.' The tearful break-up was subsequently

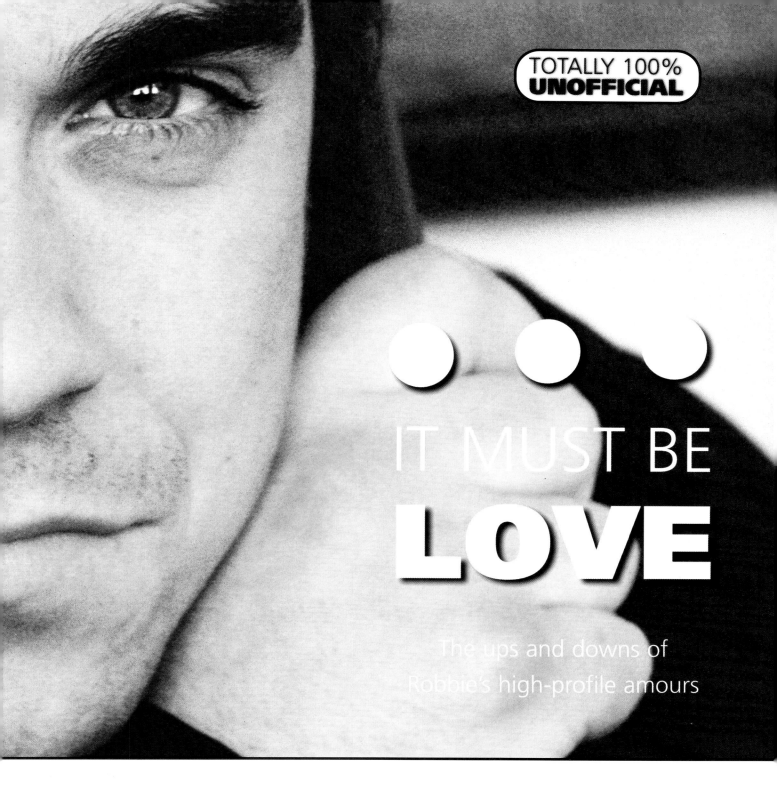

IT MUST BE LOVE

The ups and downs of Robbie's high-profile amours

blamed on the couple's frantic work schedules.

But this 'off' period was short-lived... Robbie missed Nic so much that he flew back from holiday to try and win her back. A phone call later and a declaration of affection at the V98 festival meant that the two were soon reunited. Time would only tell if they were *Back for Good*.

Sadly, things are looking a little shaky... There have been conflicting reports in the media – some sources say Robbie and Nic have split up again whilst others say they are still engaged. Whatever the case, Robbie has certainly given the media much to write about by doing what he does best... partying!

The media took great delight in reporting Rob's brief fling with Grease roadshow star Jasmine Jeffrey. Only a few weeks later the media was in a frenzy once more as Robbie had been seen getting very Up Close and Personal with dark-haired babe Andrea from the Corrs. The two enjoyed a wild night out in Dublin and it was reported that after the BRITS, Robbie sent Andrea a massive bouquet of roses with a note reading 'What do I have to do (to make you love me)?' – the title of a big Corrs hit!

Who knows what will happen next? All we know is that Robbie's young and he's having fun – and we hope that whatever he does he has 'No Regrets'!

GOING SOLO

Robbie's flight to solo stardom after the Take That era

Robbie Williams' solo career could have gone one of two ways: he could have followed the lead of either George Michael or Andrew Ridgley. During his binge year Rob met George, and told the ex-Wham! star that while everyone saw Gary Barlow as the next George Michael, Robbie planned on being the next Andrew Ridgley – in other words, a bit of a playboy. It was ironic, then, that Rob should choose to make his solo debut a cover version of George's song *Freedom*.

At the time it did look as if he was taking the Ridgley route to the bargain bin, Andrew's one and only solo effort having proved one of the poorer-selling albums of the century. At that point Robbie was on the verge of losing all his money in litigation. He felt badly about himself and his weight, and was yet to prove to himself and the world that he could write and perform songs and successfully leave the Take That years behind him.

The year out provided him with a lot of material and inspiration for writing tracks for his first album; it just took a while to come out. 'I'm actually really glad I had the court case and the management disputes because if I hadn't I'd be writing happy songs all the time.' When he finally sat down to work on the album he wrote it in seven days, the words and

music for *Angels* taking just 25 minutes.

Being back in the limelight performing *Freedom* spurred him on, as did the continued support of his mum, friends and new record company Chrysalis. They had secured him by offering a £1 million, three-album deal – but at the time weren't entirely sure what they had hold of, or even if he had any genuine talent. He was given a choice of people to work with and chose Guy Chambers, once of indie guitar-strummers World Party. The choice was as well thought-out as sticking a pin in a list, but it felt right to Robbie's gut feeling and it paid off.

Together they created a superb album in 'Life Thru A Lens'. It received great critical acclaim and Robbie finally had faith in his own abilities. 'That whole self-belief thing went out of the window for a long time, and only came back when I got good reviews for my album. That's pitiful, isn't it? But I'm confident now.' A collection of Beatle-esque guitar-rock songs, 'Life Thru A Lens' was co-written with Chambers, although Robbie writes most of the lyrics himself. 'I feel really lucky to have Guy – he's a very talented, lovely person and it's a partnership I really want to grow.'

Rob was back performing, with his own tour in ▶

GOING **SOLO**

the pipeline, and publicising the album and its respective singles to anyone who was prepared to give him coverage. Despite his best efforts, sales were disappointing. The album may have been far superior musically to Ridgley's effort, but it just wasn't selling in significant numbers. The singles were doing okay, thanks in the main part to ex-Take That fans. But young fans are not, and have never been, album purchasers. The turning point came with the spiritually-inspired *Angels*.

The previous single, *Let Me Entertain You*, had been surprising to the older audience in its sheer Rolling Stones meets Bon Jovi-esque power, but the single *Angels* made the 20- to 30-something audience sit up and take notice. Fortunately for Robbie, they then put on their coats, popped down to their local music store and bought the record. Rob had found a new audience, fans of the bands he listened to (Oasis, Pulp and their like) – and before he had a chance to realise what had happened he was hot property with a triple-platinum debut album.

With live performances, including V98, where he gave his all as a performer, he was finally accepted as a credible artist after all those years of feeling he was just a member of Gary Barlow's backing band. He had mainstream appeal, securing a more mature audience without alienating the kids. He had press acclaim, the respect of his peers, including the likes of Noel Gallagher, and as the icing on the cake he had surpassed the success of his songwriting ex-bandmate – not that such things concerned him any more.

And the success story continued with his second album, 'I've Been Expecting You'. The lead-off single *Millennium*, with its cheeky James Bond soundtrack samples, was one of those rare songs which commanded trailers from radio stations announcing its first playing, while the success of its parent album, which also went to Number 1 during November 1998, shows every sign of continuing. A string of singles were lined up for release from the album as Rob toured into the new year, and the title of the first, 'No Regrets', said it all. The time was right for Robbie Williams, solo superstar!

THE A-Z

A mass of fantastic and little-known facts on the Williams boy

A is for – Anna Friel. The ex-*Brookside* actress allegedly dated Robbie in 1997 following her failed relationship with Darren Day. Robbie maintains they always were and still are just good friends. In June '97 Rob went on a six-week rehabilitation course to sort out his drink and drugs problem. Anna was very supportive, claiming, 'He is getting better. I'm writing to him regularly.'

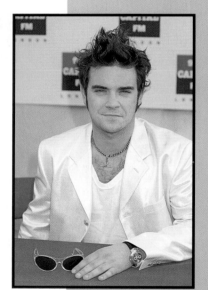

B is for – *Big Breakfast*. Robbie earned a reported £2,000 a day as guest presenter on Channel 4's early-morning programme in August 1995.

C is for – Clubs. His favourite escapes in London include Browns and celebrity hangout the Groucho Club. Regulars at the latter include Stephen Fry and the Blur boys.

D is for – Drink and Drugs. Robbie turned to celebrity therapist Beechy Colclough (who's said to have assisted Michael Jackson) to help him deal with his excessive lifestyle. Elton John, concerned about Williams' behaviour, introduced the pair, while Robbie admitted to having taken slimming pills in order to lose weight. He described his time in rehab as 'like going and having your head cleaned for a bit.'

E is for – Eccentric. Robbie's eccentricity sometimes gets mistaken for either campness or madness. 'If you're eccentric when you're young you get called mad,' he says.

F is for – French Riviera. Following his split from Take That, Robbie stayed with friends in St Tropez. Pals there included Paula Yates, the late Michael Hutchence, and George Michael, who rang him a week later to see if he was okay. He understood Robbie's predicament, having lived through the experience of being a young pop star himself.

G is for – Gallaghers and Glastonbury. Robbie was a big fan of the Oasis brothers while he was still in Take That; they invited him to join them on stage and on the tour bus when they went to the 1995 Glastonbury Festival.

H is for – Happiness. The one vital ingredient Robbie Williams claims to have added to his life since meeting Nicole Appleton.

I is for – Information and Interviews. Rob is well known for giving everything away. Sometimes he ends up contradicting himself because he speaks his mind at that moment, only to change his opinion the following week during another interview. He has a good relationship with the press and is happy to chat, wanting to be everyone's mate. The good thing about being so open is that he has nothing to hide and 'kiss and tell' stories don't concern him. 'Basically, what else could be written about me? "Robbie…Does Something Else Again"?' ▶

OF **ROB**

THE A-Z OF ROB

J is for – Jacqui Hamilton-Smith. Another of Rob's (pre-Nic) 'Angels'. Seven years his senior, they dated from November 1995 and lived together for a while. 'Posh girls always go for me – I think they find me quite amusing! They go, "Look at this peasant, a peasant who tells jokes and buys drinks!" and I fight them off with a pooey stick!'

K is for – Kylie. Ms Minogue is another in the long list of Robbie's female acquaintances.

L is for – Late Nights. After Take That, Robbie became a celebrity partygoer, attending receptions and parties across the world. He was famous for being famous and said of himself, 'I'm a bit of a social butterfly… I'm at all the parties Tara Palmer-Tomkinson's at.' Towards the end of his partying phase, he came to the conclusion that 'celebrity parties are dead boring. It's just people talking ****. I go home after ten minutes. I stay in quite a lot now.'

M is for – Mooning. At school and on stage with Take That, Rob didn't think twice before getting his bum out for the girls. An old schoolmate remembers, 'He'd always check none of the teachers were around first. After he'd done it he would say, "Don't tell my mum, she'll kill me."' One of Robbie's only half-serious ideas was to have his bum shot (as in photographed) for the cover artwork of his debut album which was, at one stage, to be called 'The Show Off Must Go On'.

N is for – Natalie Imbruglia. Another former soap star the press have linked with our Rob. He's written a song for her, too – but she reportedly declined the offer.

O is for – Orange. That's Jason Orange, remember him? The future certainly wasn't Orange in this case, as no-one's really heard of him since the end of Take That. Robbie's relationship with Jason remains slightly strained. Ironically it was Jason who'd most impressed Robbie when he first joined Take That, because he had been a dancer on late-night TV show *The Hit Man And Her*. 'We crossed wires – there was always friction between us. We were just different as people.'

P is for – Port Vale, Robbie's favourite footie team. A huge football fan, Robbie bid £16,000 at a Nordoff-Robbins Music Therapy auction in June '95, securing a seat at all Wembley matches the following season.

Q is for – Queens. 'I'm an extrovert and anybody who's an extrovert is invariably camp.' Although Robbie explains that he just doesn't swing that way, he has always found it a compliment to be 'admired' by other men. 'I don't mind men fancying me. I think it's cool to be liked by both sexes.'

R is for – Rug. And we're not suggesting Robbie wears a wig! He spent a cool £15,000 on a 50-year-old silk carpet for his mum while on holiday in Turkey.

S is for – Sporty. Melanie Chisholm apparently dated our lad for a short time.

T is for – Tim Abbot, the third, and hopefully last, manager to sue Robbie. Nigel Martin-Smith was the first, and Kevin Kinsella was the second.

U is for – UNICEF. Robbie has claimed his late-1998 UNICEF trip to Sri Lanka was 'better than Glastonbury or playing with Tom Jones at the BRIT Awards'. He visited the war-torn northern province to help publicise UNICEF's work in immunising kids against polio, accompanying Ian Dury on a celebrity mission. He told a journalist on his departure, 'I don't think I'm going to come back from this trip… I just think either I'll get shot, or I'll come back a changed man.

'I'm here because I want to put my life into place. What I worry about at home doesn't matter. I want to see how people smile in the face of adversity and carry on… I don't want to sound selfish but I do want to remember what life was like before I became famous.

'Here I'm just some white bloke making funny faces… I feel so much more serene and relaxed here. Being with those kids made me want to have my own so much… I feel I've been and done some good and I've done some good for myself too.'

V is for – Denise Van Outen. Rob was linked with the blonde, bubbly ex-*Big Breakfast* presenter before she started dating Jamiroquai's Jay Kay.

W is for – World Party. Guy Chambers played keyboards with this group before he started collaborating with Rob on his first album. Guy was also a founder member of the Lemon Trees.

X is for – XTC. Rob has recorded his own version of that group's hit, *Making Plans For Nigel*, with amended lyrics in 'honour' of Take That's manager.

Y is for – Yacht. Robbie once spent time on the French Riviera frequenting various celebrity yachts. He fell down the stairs of one, landing at the feet of Mohamed Al Fayed. 'I fell the length of the stairs, a*** over tit, and wound up in a heap at the feet of all these posh people. They're like, "Oh, the pop star Johnny's arrived".'

Z is for – Zöe Ball. One of Rob's biggest supporters. He's regularly played on her Radio 1 Breakfast Show and is a frequent guest on *Live & Kicking*.

The style and plots of Rob's wild and wacky videos to date have established him at the forefront of Brit-pop. Here's a quick trail…

SCREE
GEMS

Freedom '96
Robbie rush-released the single and had to s
video in Miami while miming to the original
Michael version.

Old Before I Die
He got to leap dramatically from a 50-foot a
Admits to certain parts of his body being lef
'chafed'.

Lazy Days
Wandered around in green, mazy *Strawberry*
type surroundings. Robbie's homage to the

South Of The Border
Claustrophobic atmosphere showing why Rc
to escape London and go back home to Mu
his 'year out'.

Angels
An ethereal video, depicting Rob in love on
and in crop circles with lots of aerial camera

Let Me Entertain You
Our hero was made up like heavy-metal king
this performance, with grotesque black and
make-up. The rockers apparently didn't appr
this imitation…

Millennium
Saw the main man all tuxed up as 'Williams,
Williams' in a Bond-style production, comple
broken jetpack.

No Regrets
Robbie walks through a backdrop of changin
and country with a dripping can of petrol fo
empty car. The finale comes when the petro
light and a line of fire traces Robbie's route.

ROB TALKS

A selection of his most outrageous quotes – and there've been many!

Rob sported a new 'blacked out' front-tooth look at Glastonbury in 1995. He said, 'I need a new image – and it'll catch on, mark my words. Kids the length and breadth of the country will have them soon.'

'I've fancied men. I've been propositioned by hundreds but I've never accepted. I take it as a compliment if a great looking girl or guy comes and chats me up.'

'I've got lots of trainers, but I don't own a house.'

'I'm sure they'll do very well. Jason, for instance, is a first-class painter and decorator.' [on Take That's future after they officially split.]

'I'm famous for being famous. I am the Amanda de Cadenet of Take That.'

'When I open the fridge door and the light comes on, I do a 20-minute stand-up routine.'

'Every time I think about the awards I get a bit nervous. I'll be an impartial host – as long as Oasis and Pulp win everything.' [on presenting MTV's European Music Awards at Alexandra Palace.]

'I mean, I'm young, daft and I've got money. Nobody can tell me what to do.'

'When four and a half million people think you're a

**** that's bad. Or you think it is. Now it's water off a duck's back 'cos I'm happy with me.'

'They're welcome to support me on tour.' [on being asked during a *Live & Kicking* interview if he saw much of the rest of Take That following the split.]

'I think the only advice I can give anybody is… don't eat yellow snow.'

'Maybe I will be assassinated one day – it would be good for record sales but I haven't got enough back catalogue yet. Maybe after the fifth album.' [on his four Italian female 'stalkers'.]

'I grew a goatee beard so that I could be attractive to goats.'

'I like beaches, too, but not sandy beaches. I have a real problem with sand – it chafes my nipples.'

'I enjoy getting my kit off. I prefer having no clothes on. I walk around the house naked; I'm more comfy that way.'

In his acceptance speech for *GQ*'s Solo Artist of the Year, Robbie thanked, 'colonic irrigation for showing me a brighter and clearer path.'

'I'm more one of those boil-in-the-bag-curry bachelor types. Curries are a great cleanout.'

DID I DO THAT?

Class clown Robbie's always been one for acting daft. Here we recall some of his silliest japes…

Robbie was always up for trouble, even as a child. When his parents ran a pub near a football ground, he took £2,000 in notes out of the till and threw it from an upstairs window into the busy street below – on a match day! He followed this up by throwing out his mother's undies…

As opposed to the standard rock cliché, Robbie threw a TV set into, instead of out of, a hotel window! He was in Ireland, picked up the telly in his hotel room on the ground floor and left the building. He then walked round and threw the set back into his room through the window and on to his bed.

He always goes skinny-dipping (nude bathing) in hotel pools. On one occasion he tried to go for a dip in the fountain in the reception area. He was a bit worse for drink and didn't realise that the fountain had been drained. He dived in and as a consequence split his head open, leaving an impressive scar.

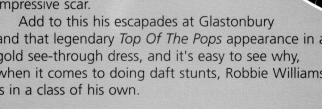

Add to this his escapades at Glastonbury and that legendary *Top Of The Pops* appearance in a gold see-through dress, and it's easy to see why, when it comes to doing daft stunts, Robbie Williams is in a class of his own.

ULTIMATE ROBBIE
MEGA-QUIZ

So just how much do you know about Robbie Williams?
Try our 20 testing questions, guaranteed to sort
out the megafans from the merely curious

1 Robbie pulled out of hosting which contest to work on his debut album?

2 In which soap opera did Robbie make an appearance as an extra after leaving Take That?

3 In which other soap did he have a bit part pre-Take That?

4 With which boy band did Robbie make a surprise appearance in Dublin seeing in the New Year in 1997?

5 Which of Rob's singles borrowed a James Bond theme?

6 What was Robbie's school nickname?

7 What was the name of the pub his mum and dad ran when Robbie was a kid?

8 What is Rob's Siamese cat called?

9 Which reading disorder does Robbie suffer from?

10 Which magazine rated Rob as Britain's second sexiest man?

ULTIMATE ROBBIE
MEGA-QUIZ

11 Why did Robbie temporarily return two platinum discs he received for sales of 'Life Thru A Lens'?

12 What is Robbie's 'year' in Chinese astrology?

13 What type of tattoo does Robbie have on his right thigh?

14 What colour are Rob's eyes? (easy one!)

15 What kind of bike does Robbie own?

16 How much weekly 'pocket money' did Robbie get when he was in Take That?

17 Robbie's most treasured possession is a signed photograph of which famous boxer?

18 What was the first single Robbie bought?

19 Robbie used to own two goldfish named after a drink: what were they called?

20 Rob made a fashion item out of which football team's shirt?

ANSWERS ON PAGE 45

ROBBIE'S ROLL OF
HONOUR

A chartography of Take That and solo hits

Take That Singles:

Do What You Like
July 1991 (Number 82)

Promises
November 1991 (Number 38)

Once You've Tasted Love
January 1992 (Number 47)

It Only Takes A Minute
May 1992 (Number 7)

I Found Heaven
August 1992 (Number 15)

A Million Love Songs
September 1992 (Number 7)

Could It Be Magic?
December 1992 (Number 3)

Why Can't I Wake Up With You?
February 1993 (Number 2)

Pray
July 1993 (Number 1)

Relight My Fire
September 1993 (Number 1)

Babe
December 1993 (Number 1)

Everything Changes
April 1994 (Number 1)

Sure
October 1994 (Number 1)

Back For Good
March 1995 (Number 1)

Never Forget
July 1995 (Number 1)

Take That Albums:

'Take That And Party'
August 1992 (Number 2)

'Everything Changes'
October 1993 (Number 1)

'Nobody Else'
May 1995 (Number 1)

ROBBIE'S ROLL OF
HONOUR

Solo Singles:

Freedom '96
August 1996 (Number 2)

Old Before I Die
April 1997 (Number 2)

Lazy Days
July 1997 (Number 8)

South Of The Border
September 1997 (Number 14)

Angels
December 1997 (Number 4)

Let Me Entertain You
March 1998 (Number 3)

Millennium
September 1998 (Number 1)

No Regrets
November 1998 (Number 4)

Strong
March 1999 (Number 4)

Solo Albums:

'Life Thru A Lens'
September 1997 (Number 2)
Lazy Days • Life Thru A Lens •
Ego A Go Go • Angels •
South Of The Border •
Old Before I Die •
One Of God's Better People •
Let Me Entertain You •
Killing Me • Clean •
Baby Girl Window

'I've Been Expecting You'
October 1998 (Number 1)
Strong • No Regrets •
Millennium •
Phoenix From The Flames •
Win Some Lose Some •
Grace • Jesus In A Camper Van •
Heaven From Here •
Karma Killer • She's The One •
Man Machine • These Dreams •
Stand Your Ground •
Stalker's Day off

FACING THE FUTURE

After all this – where next?

So the future certainly looks bright for Mr Williams. Christmas 1998 saw his new album reach many stockings, while the second and third tracks to be taken from the album as singles – *No Regrets* and *Phoenix From The Flames*, coupled as a double A-side – were among the favourites to make the Xmas week top spot. *Strong* was the third single

release, and came out the following March. There is also a tour in the pipeline for '99, with support act Divine Comedy.

He wants to collaborate with other artists and plans on writing a song with singer Tommy Scott from Liverpudlian band Space. The pair met at the V98 festival and are in discussion about a future project, but are still trying to find time to collaborate within their busy schedules.

Robbie has learned a lot from his chequered past. Proud that he stood up for himself by going through the RCA court case proceedings with three ex-managers, he nevertheless advises: 'Don't take a record company to court – settle as soon as possible and don't let lawyers have your money!'

Having lost a fortune through litigation, he is now well on track to recoup this through his solo career… but it was never the money that was important to Rob. 'I'm not worried about money as long as I can buy myself a pair of trainers and go to a restaurant every now and again. That's happiness for me!'

On the personal front he's decided to calm down and wants his own family. 'I want to be a good role model for my kids. I don't know where this father thing's come from, I've even started seeing kitchens on the telly and thinking, "Mmm, that's nice!" Five minutes ago it was motorbikes, now it's kitchens!'

So finally, how does Robbie see himself in the future? 'I don't want to be like anybody. But then I'd like to be a cross between Tom Jones, John Lennon, Chuck D and Gene Kelly. It's not much to ask for, is it?'

ULTIMATE ROBBIE MEGA-QUIZ ANSWERS

1 Mr Gay UK
2 *EastEnders*
3 *Brookside*
4 Boyzone
5 Millennium
6 Swellhead
7 The Red Lion
8 Lady Our Kid
9 Dyslexia (word blindness)
10 *Cosmopolitan*
11 There was a typing error on them, which his record company took back to have corrected.
12 Tiger
13 A Celtic cross
14 Green
15 BMX
16 £150
17 Muhammad Ali
18 *Ullo John, Gotta New Motor?* by Alexei Sayle
19 Vodka and Tonic
20 Port Vale